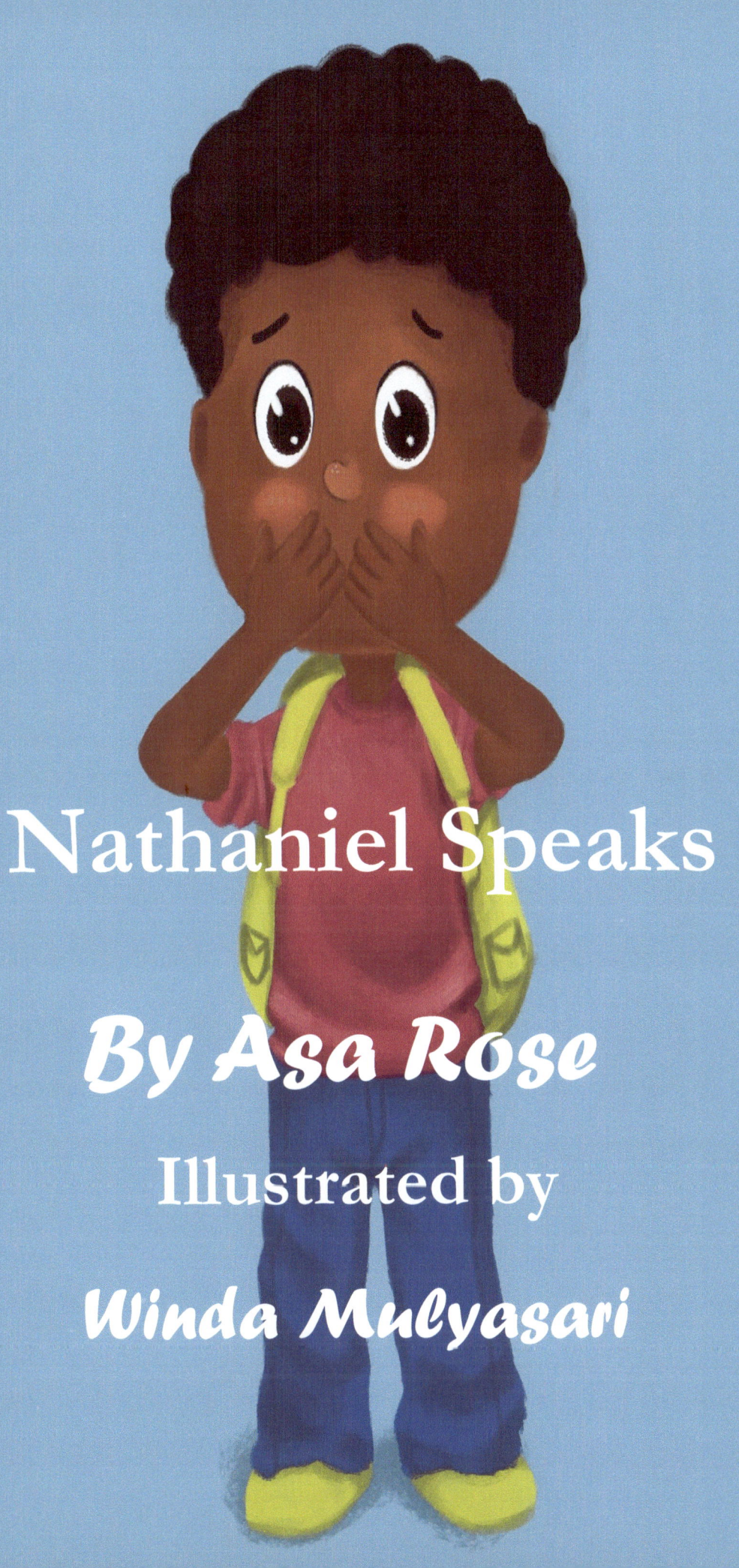

Nathaniel Speaks

By Asa Rose

Illustrated by

Winda Mulyasari

It's Monday morning and Nathaniel is almost ready for school.

He talks and plays with his little brother.

They play hide and seek...

and choose jackets with their favorite color.

Nathaniel asks his mom to pack his marble collection for show-and-tell.

At school Nathaniel's voice goes unheard.

He hasn't spoken to his friends. Not one word.

He thinks about hearing his words aloud...

but his words, just won't come out.

At story time, classmates gather around.

Nathaniel wants to choose a story but his voice, he has not yet found.

At recess Nathaniel feels very sad.

His friends hadn't heard him speak, and he wishes they had.

In silence he continues to play...

but there are still many things he wants to say.

When it is time to show-and-tell, friends volunteer.

Nathaniel knows he is brave, and wants to make a tough choice....

because he wants his friends to hear his voice.

"I have marbles!" He says.

Nathaniel's friends heard him speak aloud!

He is very proud.

He is so happy that he's going to decide,
that his voice is nothing to hide.

Lots of friends are near

and are so many things about Nathaniel
they'd love to hear!

asarosebooks@gmail.com